The Man Known As
PREI

By

PREI

authorHOUSE

1663 LIBERTY DRIVE, SUITE 200
BLOOMINGTON, INDIANA 47403
(800) 839-8640
www.authorhouse.com

First published by AuthorHouse 03/30/04

ISBN: 1-4184-0474-8 (e)
ISBN: 1-4184-0475-6 (sc)

Printed in the United States of America
Bloomington, Indiana

This book is printed on acid-free paper.

Table Of Contents

Section: God and I

Section: Life and Me

<u>God and I</u>

<u>Bring It! Or Don't Push the Christian</u>

December 20, 2002

1100

Just *who* do you think you are?

Runnin' up in my house, telling me what you're going to DO

To me—

Me,

A child of God,

He who walks in the authority of his office,

He who stands in the very place as priest of HIS house!

Who do you think you are to try to bumrush me,

Test me,

Vex my very spirit and soul with the problems of this world,

But,

Fool demon,

Hellspawn,

Fallen Angel,

It's time to put you in your place,

Under my foot!

Bam! Catch the left hook

To your jaw so you'll let go,

My money you've been holding up!

CrAcK, cRaCkLe, BREAK, and catch that,

Quick shots to the ribs,

Back up off my family, fool,

I am a Warrior!

I am a Solider!

I am a walking one man ARMY

For the Lord!

Oh, that's fine. Duck the kick,

And instead catch my *knee* to your chin,

Did that hurt? Did the sanctified *pain* of it rush through your skull?

I'll ask you again, Demon,

Devil,

You who are without hope.

Who in the heck do you think you're messing with?

Don't you know I walk with the power of JESUS in my right hand

And the backup of Angels in my left?

I'm not a hellraiser,

But I will baptize you in fire!

Get on your feet! I'm not finished with you yet!

See, you ran up in my house,

My *home*,

My CASTLE,

And now you have to pay!

So stand your feet, you festering pool of boiling hate,

And let me whoop on you until you BEG for hell's gates!

You just messed with a King,

A joint-heir to the throne of God himself,

And I'm not stopping my beat down of you,

Until He crosses heaven threshold to retrieve His children!

Get up so I can knock you down again!

Get ready for WAR!

Mj Omega

PREI

<u>Black Man Standing In The Light</u>

December 23, 2002

0940

You mock me because I stand up and fight

For the beliefs in my heart,

The thoughts in my head,

And what my soul knows to be true?

Why? Because I realize that the Bible has nothing

In it against the fighting,

As long as you realize where the fighting is to be done!

How dare you mock me for what I am,

For the I AM,

And dare to claim to understand…

When in actuality your sight is dimmed,

And blinded are you by your own ambition

To attack me,

ME, who dares to simply confess,

To stand with that understanding.

Open your eyes my brother.

Let the scales fall from your face and the light come in,

For it can let you see,

But only if you wish to.

I stand on the plain of the battlefield called the heart,

In a world called MY SELF,

And fight the demons that will plague and beguile,

And mislead,

Reaching constantly for the perfection,

For I am NOT perfect,

But one day I shall be.

I wear the mantle of CHRISTIAN not because of religion,

But because of what it means,

What it should *represent*,

"Christ-like."

Every day my Savior fought,

Though it wasn't with His fist,

But with what He did and said…

He stood on the plains of my own soul and rebuked the devil,

And all his hordes,

And He still stands there today.

What type of craziness is this,

That you would stand and speak such confusion?

Blessings and curses cannot come from the same tongue,

So take in the wisdom I've been blessed with,

And make it your own.

I'm not the best example,

But I'm still a sample.

Of what He can do.

Stand back and watch the glory unfold

From this black man standing in the light.

Mj Omega

<u>Effection</u> (first blaze of Lyrics)

December 28, 2002

0129

[yells out to the crowd]

Alright, all ya'll out there,

Time to get these pens blazin'!

Time to amaze the crowds!

But with a mellow flow…ya'll know how I do it, man…

[flows]

Stroll the streets, tryin',

To stop my folks from dyin',

Watching tears in their eyes,

Every time the sun rise,

And I'm reaching out my hands,

To help my fellow man,

But my palms are getting slapped,

Make me snatch my hands back.

But there is a question in my mind,

I ask God from time to time,

"What happened to the line,

That says all was made by thine

Hands,

And love each and every,

Man,

And we are all made the

Same,

Created in Your,

Name?"

It's caused an effect.

Now, I know the Lord didn't get it twisted.

That means that we have missed it,

So I pray,

Let my lines shine,

And give me peace mind.

Help me now to see,

Just where I need to be

To bring Your will about,

Help to bring me out,

And show me how to do,

All I can for You.

It'll cause an effect.

The Rajamalan,

Mj Omega

God is Just

January 2, 2003

1141

Do you know why Justice is blind?

Because man's concept of right and wrong

Is flawed.

What serves as "justice" for the White

Doesn't always serve as justice for the Black,

The Asian,

The Italian,

The Hispanic,

And heaven knows the Native American find justice,

To be a concept based on convenience.

Don't get me wrong; it's a good try…

But man is flawed,

So how can his laws be perfect?

But God…God IS perfection.

And when it comes to Him and justice,

It works like this:

It's JUST because HE said so,

It JUST IS,

It's JUST RIGHT,

And it all boils down to knowing and understanding

This can be because,

He's JUST GOD.

That's it. That's the point,

He said it. That settled it.

Why argue?

Just like God told Job when he dared to ask,

What right did God have to allow

Everything to be taken from him?

"Where were YOU when I created the heavens and earth,"

God said…

"Where were YOU when I set the sun in the sky?"

Understand, JUST because God said it,

That makes it RIGHT,

And JUST.

Like He told Moses when he asked,

"Who should I say sent me?"

"Tell Pharaoh that I AM THAT I AM sent you,"

Because HE is JUST GOD,

And GOD is JUST.

The Rajamalan,

Mj Omega

<u>Why Don't You Love Me?</u>

January 7, 2003

1249

What is going to take to prove my love to you?

I take care of you when you're sick,

I watch out for you all day long,

I come to visit and always bring a gift,

I give everything I can to you…

All for a simple "I love you."

All just to see you better.

All I ask is that you follow me.

You do the things I tell you to…

And it's not like those things are bad or wrong or evil,

Nah…

These are things you should do *anyway*.

They're things that will make your life better,

Will bring wealth and comfort,

Will make you a better person all around,

Filling you with love, joy and happiness,

And peace beyond anything you can imagine.

But yet and still…yet and still you turn away from me.

You mock me; you try to use me,

You look at me like I'm a joke,

You do everything you can to hurt me…

And then tell me that I don't give enough.

What more can I give? I have done everything!

Given up…everything!

I even came down to you and died by your hands,

And yet and still you can't find the strength to say, "I love you."

I've promised you a place of comfort and bliss

Once you leave the world around you.

I'm here building your mansion as we speak!

Yet you still…you still don't love me.

You'd rather burn in a place meant only for your *enemy*

Than to follow me into utter happiness.

And yet you blame *me* for your troubles.

You blame *me* because you don't have the things you want or need.

You dare to blame ME because life is too hard to bear

When I've told you I'd hold your burdens and give you my own,

Which would be nothing in comparison…

You point the finger at me every time a tragedy happens,

When that's simply *life*.

You hurt me every day, every time you reject me,

And I still love you…

But do you love me? No…no, you don't.

What will it take to prove to you

Just how much I care?

Don't you know I'd stop the world from spinning

All for you?

Why don't you love me?

The Rajamalan,

Mj Omega

<u>Vessel</u>

January 12, 2003

0722

Lord, I want to be your vessel, Father…

I want You to fill me up with You,

So that You might pore me out upon the world,

So that You might flow upon the land

From every heart to every other heart.

Take these hands, Father,

And use them to create Your work,

Take these feet, Father,

And guide me in the direction You would have me to go…

Fill my mind with Your goodness and Your mercy,

And You loving kindness,

So that I might show unto others just how strong *real* love is,

And fill my heart with Your boldness,

So that I will stand for You no matter what.

Make me into what You would have me to be,

A perfect work,

A man not only in Your image

But fill with Your power as well.

Anoint me, appoint me, and use me as You see fit,

For I am no longer my own to command or control…

I am Yours.

My spirit yearns for You, Father

It cries out for *You*, Oh God

My soul looks up into the heavens because it knows…

That's where its salvation is found.

My flesh fights and bickers with me,

Wanting to continue tasting of the world's gifts,

Oh so sweet…

But just like the sweet foods, the taste of the world is spiritually

Unhealthy.

So take me, my God, my King…You, who sit upon the throne of

heaven,

The great I AM,

And make me to be a vessel unto Yourself.

Use me, Father…until I'm all used up…

I am YOURS.

The Rajamalan,

Mj Omega

<u>Behind Enemy Lines</u>

January 30, 2003

0957

Creep along the ground, dirt all up in my face,

Skin already dark, but now buried behind lines of black grease

All for the non-detection of my presence.

Stay camouflaged.

Stealth tactics are the key.

Move silent like the wind and strike with deadly precision,

For this is a war I'm fighting in,

And I'm behind territorial lines.

Cross about my neck, under the fatigues,

True silver, just a piece to remind me of my faith.

That faith is the only thing that keeps me going,

That and being blessed to live to see this day…how much longer…

That's what I find myself wondering, how much longer

Until death finally seals me up and sends me off to my reward,

Judgment for heaven or hell.

Almost there, though already so deep behind the lines,

I've lost sight of the others. The darkness is too deep.

Keep moving. Keep pushing. Been trained for this.

I'm a solider, I'm a fighter, I'm like the warriors of old,

Trained for group combat,

And the battlers of today, an army of One.

All rolled up together…highly skilled and specialized…got one purpose,
One single-minded goal.
And I'm almost there.
Been lying low for days, moving like grass roots,
Slowly.
But now…now it's just about time for the plan to unfold and us to show
Just what we can do…it's almost…
Now!
Now I stand up and rise from the filth of the ground and lift my hands
And let free my soul…whose light shines across the land and connects
With the others that were creeping behind the battle
To shed the light of Christ upon the devil's land…made a move and took it
Back!
Made a motion and showed all that He is Lord and through us…through His military,
He has redeemed a land forsaken!
Smiling as I settle down, light still shining but no long blinding,
Smiling because I had the faith to step behind enemy lines,
Smiling because I might not be promised the battle, but I am promised the war,
Yet I/we have won again.

The Rajamalan, Mj Omega

<u>Life and Me</u>

<u>Ramifications</u>

December 29, 2002

0250

Every time I close my eyes and look back,

The memory still burns me,

Eating away at flesh and skin,

But mostly at my emotions.

My head becomes a whirlwind of feelings,

And I have to cry out in pain over what I see…

Viewing my memories in the third person,

Pain felt in the first.

You pursued me like a fox hunts a lamb

But found you had a tiger by the tail…

You sought me till, finally, I turned and descended

Down into the depths of your soul,

Your heart,

And your flesh.

How sweet was the taste!

The things we did and shared back then,

The problems we faced, both real and pretend,

Served to acknowledge what we shared.

Separated by distance,

Bonded close by love…

But worse yet was how I was fooled and misled,

23

Damaged by what most would have viewed as damaged goods.

But not me…oh, no, my heart…damnable thing that it is,

Wouldn't let me just sit by and watch as yours died.

And I reached, I pulled, I clawed, I struggled,

Until from the depths you rose like a phoenix…

I was your first "I love you,"

I was your first truth…

All glory goes to God, but *I* was the instrument…

And I was sorely misused.

See, for every "I love you" I gave,

I found out that there was another,

Behind the scenes…

Working like a bloody maggot to get in

And finding access!

Until that time came when you finally could stand on your feet,

And you walked away from me.

I stood against all odds,

From my SKIN to my AGE,

And yet you walked away from me.

You were so ready to believe the worse,

That I couldn't love you after all you told me about you…

And I proved to you that it was a lie, again and again,

That this heart…ah, God, this heart…could take in all you were,

And still see all you could be,

And yet you walked away from me.

Ouch.

Ouch, damn it!

You asked me once, if I left,

To close the door to your heart softly;

Yet when you turned from me, you kicked mine in…

What a way to be. Made me feel like a turned trick.

Tell you what, dearest, do this…

Keep going. And don't look back…

I won't be here.

The Rajamalan,

Mj Omega

PREI

A Moment

January 13, 2003

1543

I see the sun, the sky, and the clouds in the vast expanse

Of big blue openness…

Leaning my head back like a child does

When running in the park sometimes…

Or playing in the rain.

It's like looking into the soul of the earth,

Staring at the sky like this;

My heart reaches out and touches

Every other part of nature,

And I become one with everything,

Master of all I see.

Is it vanity that moves me so?

Perhaps.

But let me have that.

Let me let go while I stare up into the sky,

Crystal clear and blue…

Let me pretend that I am a bird flying,

Or a buzzing bee,

Or sunlight…

Let me be free for that moment,

For I am a poet…I realize that this flesh that holds me,

Is more of a prison than anything else,

Of my essence, my soul.

And my soul…longs to be free.

So, you let me have this moment of vanity,

If that's what it is,

This moment of being totally happy,

While I become a child again, staring happily up

At the sun, the sky and the clouds.

The Rajamalan,

Mj Omega

The Path I Walk

January 13, 2003

1708

This path I'm on was so lonely,

But no longer.

Now there walks beside me a helpmate,

Stronger than I am spiritually

Yet depending on me for guidance.

I carry twin pistols by my side

And a sword on my back

She carries combat knives,

Just in case,

Incase our enemies run up on us,

And I'm overwhelmed…

In case there is a hold up on the blessings

That keeps us going…

She's got my back, and I've got hers

On this path we walk.

The Rajamalan,

Mj Omega

PREI

Be Whomever You Want to Be

January 14, 2003

1504

Quit trying to be like all the people around you

That are so popular, so in the public eye,

Or so surrounded by fake friends that are only there

Because they're destine to be followers.

Be yourself. Be whatever it is you want to be.

Don't be bound up in tradition,

Though I wouldn't recommend doing away with it totally

Some things help to build foundations,

But once you have that, stand on your own two feet.

If you care to speak boldly, then learn when you should

And when you shouldn't,

And do so as you see fit…

If you want to wear your clothing a certain way,

Be my guess…but don't look at me like I'm wrong

Because I might not like it. That's me, and you're you,

Be whoever you want to be.

In this world we all walk on paths that run

Beside others and sometimes cross or combine;

You must find your niche, your place, your identity,

If you plan to exist at all here…

So, forget what other's say. You be you, and I'll be who ever,

Whether that happens to be a person alone or with someone,

Well liked or not…

It's better than being a clone.

The Rajamalan,

Mj Omega

<u>This Is The Way I Am</u>

January 15, 2003

0909

I can walk on the surface of things,

Like Christ did upon the water that time,

Both guns at my side, ready to blaze in various styles,

Or…

I can reach down into the depths of my very life

And yank from my soul a portion of what I am

To spread around and hopefully touch someone

Right in the center of their being.

But either way, that's just me.

Part of the spectrum that represents this rainbow,

Called by various affectionate names.

It's all a part of me.

Like a diamonds facets,

I let others glimpse me in various degrees

Of intensity.

I can walk along on the earth,

Dropping lead words from my guns

Into the chest of my adversaries and friends alike,

Each with different results.

Or…

I can rise up gently upon the currents of living

And draw on the sun that I call my heart

So that I might rain down like sunlight,

Something pure that hits everyone

With no respect of person, as it should be.

Yet it reminds me.

Like water rushes along at various speeds,

From gentle to destructive,

I move in varying waves,

Sometimes crashing against the shore,

Sometimes just running along the sand.

But it always reminds me, the unique being,

That God fashioned in the warmth of my mother

To be whatever it was I am to be…

It'll always be me.

The Rajamalan,

Mj Omega

Ill Flow

January 15, 2003

0944

There is a flow going through the world today

That says to the brain and heart and soul

That it's okay to cross any line you see

As long it pleases you…however briefly.

It says, "Cut if you feel like it, get it, hit it,

And kick the trick to the curb,"

To the fellas,

And to the ladies it says, "This is all you're worth.

Spread your legs and let him in. Please this man

Though you can look in his eyes and know he doesn't want you,

Just the hole you've got to put his dick in."

It rubs me the wrong way to see everyone walking around

With death in their eyes because their souls have died,

And they've been buried for various reasons

Under the cost of living in today's society.

The problem lies in both male and female hands,

For one doesn't respect because the other doesn't ask for it,

And the other doesn't ask for it because the other doesn't give.

Like hamsters captured in a spinning wheel, we run,

In a constant circle of self confusion,

Letting the induction of money for a lyrical pattern

And a tight flow,

Lead us to think that it's okay to call our women bitches

And our men something less than that.

Oh, sure, we've managed to dull the blow of the word,

Whites put upon us

By saying it to each other in a ribbing type fashion…

But the sting of it still remains,

And if we're not careful that that we say lightly,

Will fall heavy upon the heart and mind.

I'm like Outkast on ATLiens,

"It disgusts me to see my folk run up on,"

Which is just what's happening, now from the inside out,

After fighting so hard to keep it from happening from the outside in.

We beat upon each other in various ways,

Crushing the ambitions to be better than we present ourselves

Because "that's playing the white man's game"

Open your eyes, *nigga*.

They've got the money and the foot on your throat,

And you've got your hands on their ankle keeping it there, holding it down,

To make sure you die not of prejustice,

But of self-ignorance.

And this thing with my sistas and their hair,

Laced with blond streaks that you know you weren't born with.

Hey, some of you all look cute like that,

And some of you look like fifty-cent whores.

Look in the mirror and see the beauty you really possess

Before deciding to buy into the image…

Which is what I see as the problem.

It's not the music with its tight flows and rhymes

It's the mentality behind it.

So what if you're talking about what you've really been through

Or what so many of us experience…

Be my guest. I'm a poet, and that's all I do,

Write about what I know, feel, see, etc.,

But now it's cool to be poor, cool to be stupid,

And to act not the *nigga* but the *nigger*…We've got rich folk running around

As though they're ghetto fab,

Never been there a day in their life!

It's hard to knock some things about the way we do things,

But changes have got to be made if we're to survive…

I think with all the ranting my soul is doing,

I'll start here, with me…and work on myself…

Every revolution started with one mind, one idea, one voice to speak,

And one person willing to change.

The Rajamalan,
Mj Omega

Attempted Robbery

January 16, 2003

1700

You came over across the seas,

In your boats, sails unfurled in all your

Unholy glory.

Like a plague of locust you swept into the land,

Lies out your mouth at first,

Truth told later when you put us in chains,

Or the lead into our bodies.

Murderers. Liars. Takers of things

That no one has a right to take.

You see something you want,

And because you feel…you have some *right*,

You remove those that own it

To claim it for yourself.

What causes your souls

To be so dark and while your skin is so light,

I'll never know.

Talking about how good you are

While treating those of us with a *tint*,

As though we're less than you.

There will be hell to pay. Can you stand the debt you've

accumulated?

I speak as the Black,

And the Native,

And the Mexican,

The Cuban,

Hispanic,

And so on and so forth…for you even fight your own kind.

Now you wonder why we don't like you,

Why we distrust you,

Why we harbor hate at times within ourselves.

Because you're so…good.

It's hard to look into your eyes and not find

Some reason to detest you…

Though I've never been taught to hate,

I have been taught caution.

Some of you dare to say that this place

No longer holds that dirty word racism

In it's vocabulary.

Strange how that can be

When I face it every day.

I've heard you scream that we should go back where we come from

When you brought us here in the first place.

Sick it is how you look upon me with defilement

Because my eyes hold the fire of hope in them…

A hope you can't take from me.

I will walk with pride because I refuse to let

Your attempted robbery succeed.

You can't take what I am from me...

But you *will* have to deal with it. I'll see to that.

The Rajamalan,

Mj Omega

Trying

January 17, 2003

1130

You know what I'm fed up with?

Ignorance.

Statements like this: color doesn't matter anymore.

Tell me, what world do you live in,

Wherein my skin tone doesn't affect

The view those with less of it place upon me?

Or even the view I have of *them*?

Because that place must be PARADISE,

And not on earth.

Don't get me wrong.

It's not something that's going to control me.

I've been sun-kissed a long time,

So I've learned to cope and deal and to

Live.

The way I see it is that those that hate must be jealous

Because as much as they pick at my brown color,

They stay in the sun trying to achieve it.

That makes me laugh, and the laughter

Eases the pain.

I walk in the grace that God has given me

And believe that no matter what this world holds against me,

I can still make it with His help.

But I'm not blind to the fact that I'm treated differently,

Trusted less,

And looked upon as less…

Sometimes I even have to stop myself from doing it back to those

That deliver it upon my doorstep.

I keep telling myself I have to be better,

That they're loosing out because they can't take the time

To know the man within the flesh of black heritage.

And I make it. Daily I struggle through it and I make it

And feel GOOD about myself when I go home.

But I can't ignore it. I can't pretend it's not there

I can't behave as though I don't know the history of our peoples,

Who owned who, why and when…

Because I do know. My blood still remembers…

And my flesh wants to hate for the hate that was delivered

For no other reason except we exist.

But my soul knows better…and it stays in control.

Yet I will and can stand, even if defiantly,

Just to prove the fact that though I know what's happened

Though I remember the past, deal with the present and look forward

To the future,

I'm still something and someone everyone will have to deal with,

Me and my blackness.

The Rajamalan,

Mj Omega

<u>Beauty Unseen</u> (a simple song)

January 19, 2003

1505

(Verse 1)

Staring out my window,

At the world below me…

Looking at the sky,

The world so blue above me…

My eyes fill with tears,

Cause my heart, it fears,

It'll never see such beauty

Again…

(Verse 2)

Watching as the sun rises

Over the trees…

Feeling the warm light

Washing over me…

My soul sings out,

Because it knows without a doubt

I'll never see such beauty,

Again…

(Chorus)

It's all about love…

That is what I see when I look around.

It's all about love…

It's even in the rain that's coming down,

And it's the very sand beneath my feet

Because the God that made me,

Made this world out of the beauty,

Of love.

(Verse 3)

Looking in my wife's eyes,

And she's looking into mine…

Smiling like a school child

Because of the way they shine…

And I cry at our love.

I know we're blessed from above,

And I'll never see such beauty,

Again…

(Verse 4)

No, there's nothing in the world

That can make me feel like this does…

And I'll never see,

Never see…

I'll never see such beauty…
Again.

The Rajamalan,
Mj Omega

PREI

Hot Pursued Damnation

January 22, 2003

0911

Pursued me, you did,

You came after me.

You sniffed the air like a predator

And caught my scent,

Then set me up with sex and seduction.

Eighteen and blindsided I was by your approach,

Overpowered by the waves of emotions I felt,

Confused by the emptiness that beat within your chest,

And caught up in the trap you had laid.

I was yours. Totally.

For you I would turn my back on everything,

All that I knew,

Because you told me that you didn't know what love was…

That an evil man's childhood act had stripped such a thing from you,

And now…now "I love you" didn't fit the vocabulary.

It didn't sound from within your being.

You were hollow.

But you…you opened a door in order to catch me and ensnared

yourself,

For I stood there in all my God-given power

And flooded your soul with all that I was feeling for you,

49

That youthful, unabashed, untouchable emotion,

That purity of love unscarred,

I gave that to you despite everything…

I proved my words by my actions, as any man should do.

And I did that, because I knew that I loved you.

Your loving was off the chain,

Left me shook, unhooked, and highly erotified,

But the love itself was sweeter still…that's what I craved,

And longed for.

Fast forward.

We've been at it for months now; at least I have,

Fighting against your unsurities,

Re-affirming my commitment and love to and for

Only you.

Yet you pushed and pushed and pushed me away further each day,

Killing me softly with kind words that really mean

I don't want you, and *you're not what I need.*

Now that the restoration is done and you can breath again,

You've finally exhaled and behind my back said the words

That you could barely say to me!

You whispered and crept and finally slipped backward,

And preferred that he come to the rescue rather than me…

Perhaps I didn't see the signs.

Maybe I didn't pay attention.

All I know is this: I opened the door to your heart,

While you tore the soul out of mine,

And I let the death happen…because I believe in love

While you believed in loving another.

And you wondered why I couldn't talk to you.

You WONDERED WHY I couldn't stand to be around you and

him…

You actually WONDERED why my heart shut you out so completely

While I died constantly and repeatedly,

For your seeds of hell had come up with *fire*,

And the smoke was choking me to death.

And now you wonder why people tell you I cry myself to sleep

And don't bother to wash the tears away in the morning…

Let's just say I'm testifying to a love that burned like fire.

Unknown to me, they were the fires of damnation.

The Rajamalan,

Mj Omega

My World

January 23, 2003

1042

Cars parked in the lot, settled in like sheep or cattle,

Buildings standing silent and forlorn.

Desolation is the key to being here.

The sun shines brightly down on the nothingness of unanimated

objects,

Reflects harshly off the roof tops of metal

While inside we sit, trapped in our offices,

Looking out of windows.

Looking outside from within.

Looking…out.

Wishing all the while that this wasn't necessary,

That things would just fall into place and that we could live not

easily…but happily.

Fingertips pressed against the glass, wish-building steadily,

Fed up with the normalcy,

Choking on the redundant silliness of having to complete meaningless

tasks,

Lack of importance placed on the shoulders, weighing down,

But still pressing…to be free.

Went from picking cotton to filing papers,

From having nothing to having some change…

But never enough to exceed expectations,

Never enough to succeed.

Education built upon curiosity, the need to know more than currently

acknowledged,

Fingers still pressing the glass

Like buttons on the keyboard that moves the words from the brain to

the screen,

Wondering for school, wishing for better, painting landscapes like

great artist

Of past times and lives gone by, feeling locked down,

Life going by…

Life *passing* by, leaving without picking up one of the passengers,

That treasure it the most.

Roaring in the ears, fingers still pressing,

Pressure building while Michael Jackson irritates from the CD,

Another distraction to the dream of being *free* from this…

Never wanting much, just some comfort, a break from the common,

But stuck in the commonplace.

Fingers pressing…constantly begging for the release,

Glass resisting but for how long?

How long will the confinement hold before the anger builds,

Before the longing becomes too great and like a sledgehammer to a

brick wall,

It begins to get chipped away,

Bit by bit until…

Fingers pressing…*thru,* passing out while the glass shatters and I
fall…

Plummeting down to rock bottom…

Been here before, though, climbed back up into my office building,

Locked myself back down to get regrounded and gain sure footing…

Longing to be free again and finally dropping the restraints.

Time to fly, no more falling, rise like the eagle and finally become…

Free.

The Rajamalan,

Mj Omega

Urban Inspiration

January 25, 2003

2019

Just a few lines in order to help everyone's spirits lift,

A few words to help the downtrodden heart realize

That it's not all over yet…it's just beginning.

It's all in how you open your eyes and view the things around you.

Yeah, there are bullets on your block.

There are thugs that carry heat and fling it like water flings

Out of the tub at bath time,

But you can dodge the bullets.

You can skip by and walk over the traps and snares.

I'm not talking about your flesh, brothers and sisters.

I'm not talking about this skin and bone that can be so frail.

I'm talking about your spirit. I'm talking about your soul.

Two parts of you in a tri-living being.

Which part will rule?

Will you fall into the trick of the devil, pick up the guns, throw lead?

Or will you learn to pick up the Bible and learn how to be alive

Instead of the living dead?

If your soul is poetic, will you pick up your pen and pervert the gift,

Writing words that mislead like many do?

Or will you let your pens be your weapon against oppression

And use them to script the lines that will cut through darkness

Like blades dipped in the blood of Christ?

It's all on you.

See, there is a whole lot of talk,

Very little action

That goes on.

Everyone has something to say, everyone has something to speak about,

But what are you doing?

Are you at least living the life that says, "I don't HAVE to be like this

I don't HAVE to be your stereotypical individual

I walk to a higher calling."

Life is in your hands,

And no matter what anyone says, they can't take it from you.

You can face down .45's if your heart is in the right place,

Because you'll know it's just one part of you they can reach…

Your soul can fly forever.

Nice words and condolences, I know that's what it sounds like I'm saying,

But I've got a question for you: how do you know I'm not speaking real?

How do you know that I'm not feeling in my heart the same rage you do,

Over the blood in the streets spilled by the hands of our own and others,

Over family lost in the struggle?

Take the chance; lift your head,

Take the lead and walk forward.

Hope I reached you this time, before it's too late for yet another.

Hope I climbed into your heart and tapped out a message

That'll stick to your mind and vibrate your insides

Until like the rushing water they speak of in the Bible,

It pours back out of you, living and pure,

Message spread again.

Wonder where I got my song from?

Wonder where these words that fill my heart and leap out of my hand

To the page in front of me,

And from the page to you?

Wonder how my pen became the very instrument that nailed Jesus to
the cross,

Shedding His precious blood?

How that self same pen became His tool for spreading everything

He's put in me?

Open your Bible, read the Book…His death was for me and for you,

So it's just like I killed Him…and yet He loves me.

Learn before you object me.

Open just a bit and see if it's real before you dismiss.

Try and see if there is another way, if there is truly a help to make it.

See if I'm really speaking with Urban Inspiration.

The Rajamalan,

Mj Omega

Finally Got Me Mad

February 4, 2003

0910

I hate people lording over me, whether in authority or not,

For I give respect to be treated *with* respect,

And granted, not all will return that to you…

But I don't know…

Some people just grate your nerves so intensely,

They are so aggravating that it grieves your soul,

And flips the switches that say retaliate!

Return fire! Show this fool who he's messin' with!

But no…no…one must remain in control,

Cool, calm, resistant to the outside pressures.

And I am, usually…I am…

But one day, I fear so great that it vexes me constantly,

Somebody will push all the buttons; break the control panels…

And finally just royally piss me *off.*

I feel for this person that does…I really do. They have no idea

The type of trouble they're getting themselves into.

I KNOW my anger…I know what it drives me to do,

I know the history of my family, of the uncontrollable ones,

Those that ride the jail system because every time they get angry,

They snap. That's in my bloodlines.

Be it except for my family and the teachings and things I learned
growing up poor,

I would have surely been one of them.

For I am *volatile* when I get like that…violence is not the way to
describe what happens,

Destruction is a better term.

But I wait…I digress…I breath and I point this thing in me in another
direction,

Funnel its passion into a flirtatious infectious nature,

Make myself be the nice guy with smart-aleck comments,

Turn my anger into passion and my passion into words, deeds and
actions,

I make myself move from satan's dragon to God's lion,

Though it wasn't always that way. Though I didn't always walk on
the Lord's side,

With calm discretion. His hand has kept me even then, so I give to
Him all,

And I fight my anger, I control it, I use it to build a better *me…*

And pray against the day somebody finally pushes me too far.

The Rajamalan,

Mj Omega

__Introduction__

February 6, 2003

1458

Stealth whispers on the wind, movement like shadows,

There is no light except for that which is in my eyes.

Focus. Must stay sharp and on task,

Annoyed by distractions…things to lead me away from the set path,

I walk. I step, quietly, moving along at my own pace,

Guidance given to a soul wounded by simply living.

How to heal, how to breathe…how to move forward from standing

stagnant

To standing above all. How to *fly*, given the chance to shine now,

To break free from obscurity into the light that can be blinding,

Light that can sear a man unprepared from going to long unnoticed.

Mustn't be indifferent, mustn't standing alone,

But stand ahead of the crowd, be a point that breaks that wall ahead,

Stand on the cutting edge…rank of General in God's army.

Looking, seeking, heading toward something different,

Toward *being* different…than I am…

Never lose that essence, no, I won't…

But I can't stay like this forever.

Time to change, time to move, let the pens stand up stronger than

swords

And twice as sharp. Let them *bite* when they're heard,

Cut twice as deep. It's time for the words to not only have life but animation.

Resurrection as happen within me…Long dead passions have arisen. Long dead feelings have been stirred,

For I see…I see! New things have been birthed in me and constant evolution has begun.

Welcome to the new me.

Prei

Black American

February 7, 2003

1251

I have no homeland to go back to…no place that holds my heart

I am not an African…I have never been there. I was not born…there.

All I know of is America.

All I've been is…American.

Be that good or bad, this is my *home*.

I share my home with people from all over the world

And every day I leave the real dream of America…the truth behind it

Despite what *man* as brought, wrought, and done.

In this land I am free…moreso than in any other. Hard fought

freedom.

Freedom that is not yet totally reckoned but closer

Than when we started. In this land I hold hands

With men, women, boys, girls,

From every color of the rainbow…

And I stand against everything that is wrong…in America.

I stand against its twin tongue that says you may succeed

But only if your skin isn't tinted,

Against it's motto that says, "Send me your huddled masses,"

When it means "Keep them to yourself."

I stand against the foot of oppression that is on every neck from

everybody,

Even those whose tones are lighter than mine.

I pledge myself to them all…to this land represents so much good

And so much bad.

I pledge myself to my home. Not to all its dictates…not to all its

decisions

But to what it should have always been,

Land of the *free,*

Home of the *brave.*

Prei

Circumstances

February 7, 2003

1535

Standing here, looking at the gun, at the brother behind it

There is no fear in his eyes. There is no *life* there.

Thinking I'm a dead man, my mind races through life.

Did my sanctification bring me here? To this point? To death?

I think not. I drop my hands and watch the man's eyes, silent

It's a test of my faith now…a test of whether or not I truly believe

Or am I just running my mouth?

He asks for the wallet. It's given. He asks for the watch, given too.

He asks for the chain and the rings and the shoes…all given, freely.

He watches me because I'm expressionless…screams out loud "What
are you looking at?"

Face doesn't change as I reply "The very man Christ died for."

Cold stare…ice in the eyes…but warming. Backing off of me as life
begins to eat up his death.

Soul thawing out slowly as he runs…I realize I have lost little in the
encounter

And he gained much. A seed, planted and growing now waits for
water. For harvest.

All it cost was some money that He gave me…and a few things He
blessed me to buy.

Prei

<u>Special</u>

February 10, 2003

2358

She looked at me, silent for so long.

I soon started to believe that there was a problem…

Whispered to her I did, asked what's the matter.

Why was she staring, why was she watching?

What was she watching for?

Smiling was the reply, no speech.

Never was a word said while she got up and approached me.

Mind raced with thoughts of confusion.

What had I done? Was this trouble or good?

Sweet kisses were given, briefly but repeatedly.

Lips were touched against another's with pleasure beyond the mere

contact,

For souls reached out each time, embraced

Touched and became one, then parted again,

Two halves that existed in close proximity

Enjoying the ecstasy of oneness.

Words parted finally, reasons were given for the look in her eyes

For the meeting of our eyes…

For the staring in *my* eyes that she was doing,

Looking me over like I was some treasure beyond measure to be had

by her

Without making me feel like less than I am…but rather more than I

dreamed I

Could be.

She kept looking and finally whispered, finally said with soft tones

and gentle speech,

"You'll never know how special you are to me…

You have no idea just how special you are to me…

You are *special* to me. I love you."

All I could think in the rapture of emotion that followed and blushed

In my brown-skin cheeks was this:

I'm special. Special Me.

Prei

Two Pieces to the Puzzle

February 17, 2003

0953

God created both men and women

But He did NOT create them equal.

Though He could have, He chose instead

To make us different, unique.

Imagine if you will, a man and a woman,

Both created the same way, in the same form,

The same likeness of each other.

I doubt the "woman" would have been named Eve

But rather "Steve"

And homosexuality would not be a sin

Because there would truly be no women in the first place.

But in His infinite wisdom, God created a being in His image

And upon looking at him decided that

It wasn't good for man to be all by himself

And made another being in the image of what God would want as a

companion

To give to us, men, as a gift that can only be surpassed

By God's love for us.

Read the Book. We were all created in His image

But for a different purpose. One came from the dust

The other came from the rib

But both are meant to walk WITH each other

Not one beneath the other.

And that's the problem that I see…not that women want to be equal

But they just want to stand there with us.

Let's admit, in some things men are better

And in some women must take first place

But all of us should be treated fairly, with respect, love, kindness,

Dignity.

That's the point that should be made: the Book's golden rule spoke aloud

Do unto others as you would have them do unto you.

We men are a piece in the puzzle, but only a piece.

Women are the other…and you know what?

Without one piece, the puzzle remains incomplete.

Without ONE PIECE, things are left undone.

WITHOUT ONE piece, wholeness cannot be reached, truly

Making both important in different aspects

Not so one can look down upon the other

But so that both can walk together, side by side,

Made not to be equal

But to fit together equally.

Prei

Black History

February 18, 2003

0914

This is Black History month,

Shortest month of the year

Even shorter is the memory of what's gone on.

So many uneducated and have succumbed

To the notion that all the struggling has been

In vain. We complain about what's not right today

Without doing anything about it,

Saying to ourselves, "I refuse to do it the right way

So I'll slang these drugs, I'll sell myself,

I'll corrupt God's gift of my LIFE in order

To earn this green paper that makes the world go 'round."

Forgotten is the fact that it was harder when our parents

And grandparents

Were younger and stronger

And given less…worked with less

Yet held on to God and somehow made it.

Easily we give into the image of the "thug" mentality,

Thinking that's the way to be, the way to make it,

Forgetting we're God's warriors and not the world's vagabonds.

We feel the pride of black blood in our veins but refuse to be men and

women

Under the One that put it there.

Christ was black in my opinion, yes…

Hard to hide a white-skinned, blue-eyed child amongst Egyptians

But does it matter? All that matters is the love and the sacrifice

Things we as a people have forgotten,

Sacrifices made for us from the time Jesus died until now,

Sacrifices still being made but unknown

Just to keep us moving forward, bit-by-bit…

We didn't have the freedom to complain, but now we do it readily,

Didn't have a choice to look a white man in the eyes and tell him he's
wrong.

Now we dare someone to violate us and not catch retribution

But we've forgotten what it took to get us here…forgotten the lessons
learned.

If we're not careful, our freedom will be forgotten as well

Unless we remember what it took.

Remember Black History.

Prei

<u>Stroke</u>

February 22, 2003

0627

My bed is calling me

Cause my wife lays there…

And it's not for the beauty she possesses or

Her prowess in our playground that is only matched

By me.

But right now, I'm missing my baby's touch.

So soothing, like a cool towel on the fevered forehead

Or being tucked in at night, deep beneath the covers.

I long to feel her close, but I can't

I won't…

Because she's sleeping.

She's resting like I wish to do but can't

Because of this poetic drive in my head.

It's got me sitting up with a need to bang out words

Though I have yet to be able to form a solid thought.

Zombie like, I sit, dazed, sleep taking and releasing me,

Waving in the chair yet still writing

The pool is stirring, and like that one of Old Testament days

I must get in while the water's troubled.

Feeling not up to par as wishes to dream and float in the realms

Between death and life, where my soul hangs in the balance,

I wish to chat with angels and slay some demons

But not until my soul releases me from this poetic flowing…

Seems I'm doomed to be this way for life

But I don't complain…there are harder gifts to maintain, to hold

More difficult things to work in.

Instead I have been chosen to speak that which is inside of me,

Expressively and poetically…learn from my mistakes and keep growing

Though I sure wish I could go sleep with my wife

On time, at the right time…

And feel her lull me into the cradle of rest with a simple touching of her hand,

Love's stroke.

Prei

United I Stand

February 23, 2003

2355

My heart is weeping, deep inside

Sorrowful tears flow from my chest.

My eyes scream up at Heaven

Why? Why must we suffer?

Transported back in time, my mind has been

And I see the strange fruit hanging from the trees.

I hear the screams of my sisters raped, screams unheeded

Because everyone is running for their lives.

Hate runs amuck in the hearts of men

Separated by the colors of skin though the bone is yet white

And the blood is yet red.

Watching as my people are beaten, bruised and buried

With the bodies of those that have already been hung

And burned.

And I know what HATE is.

I feel it pound in my heart and I want to give it sway.

I cry because I want to let it run through me like it runs though those

That dare to say this is right…

Mocking the name of Christ

By calling yourself Christian.

You're anything but! Fouling the belief for my people

Because all they can see is how you act

While claiming Christ as your Savior.

So much runs through my heart…purely evil thoughts,

Wondering how to return the violence dealt to my bloodline…

Closing eyes, praying…I know where MY help comes from

And He is the only one that will deliver me from the pain I'm feeling,

Realizing that hate grows by spread hatred

And that the only way to heal is to love…

Makes me wonder why Love is so powerful

Till my mind opens and my heart beats

And my soul wraps around this concept:

Love hurts. Love HURTS.

Whipped and beaten, bleeding while being nailed through the wrist

To a piece of wood, uplifted and displayed

Having the power to call down the host of heavens to save oneself

Yet not doing it…dying…burial…resurrection with all power.

Heaven promised to those that would simply believe, follow and tell others

LOVE did that. Nothing else but LOVE.

Commanded to love my enemies, I realize just how much I must do,

How big I must be,

How strong my soul must become…

Transported back to the present, back to my time

Looking around, hearing sounds, and taking a sniff,

I can tell hate still exists…

Quieter…maybe even deadlier because of that

But it's still here.

Returned home, picked up the pen and started writing…

Started pouring out everything I felt building inside

Then decided to make my mark, my difference…

Begun reaching out, despite color, despite creed

Poetic heart to poetic heart and to those that read the scripts

Locked spiritual hands with others of my calling

Stood with them on a new frontier…

I stood with the rainbows of the nations

I still stand today.

And I know I've done so little…so very little

But with faith, I know it will make a difference.

Someday, some child will read the words scripted here.

That child will read my heart and know…

That hatred can be stopped.

Prei

Parchment

February 25, 2003

2345

A soul is birthed, blank but with a destiny

That being to be scribbled upon by life.

It grows and goes forth into the world,

Getting etched upon by experiences,

Drawn on by life's twists and turns.

Doodles are left in its corners by emotions.

These are the things that make it up

And make us who we are.

My soul has many writings upon it,

Erasers marks here and there from hurts grievous

Removed, recovered from, written over

But not forgotten.

I take a line from here and there and weave them

With poetry in mind

Into something to impress upon the minds of others.

I use my heart as a pen to write upon other souls

To leave my marks within them, whether they be great or small,

Few or many.

There is space on my soul for you…leave your mark.

Write your name upon me…you won't fade the whiteness

Of the light shining from within me.

You won't damage me beyond repair…I invite you,

Implore you even.

Leave your mark upon me. Write what you would have me to

remember

Of you

Upon this soul of mine, my book of life.

Drop the drops of your living ink upon its pages…

Feel free to do so.

But don't get blinded by its brightness, for I glow with the light

Of a million stars…a million dreams…a million memories.

I live for the experience…for the taste of love

Of friendship, of caring

Of hurt

Of despair

Of sadness.

I live to be alive and to one day walk the streets of Glory

With my life's written text in my head,

A pen in my hand

And another soul to write upon.

Leave your mark upon me.

Prei

Rain Fall

March 17, 2003

1248

Have you ever just at and watched the rain come down?

A slow, steady drizzle,

Or a tormented downpour…

The way the sky turns gray like the wrath of God

Or the sun keeps shinning while soft droplets hit the ground.

It's beautiful…it's unique.

The lightning flashes like a bravado, silent but frightening

Followed by the roaring of the thunder

Sounding so loud that it shakes buildings

With mere sound vibrations.

You can see the building of the white, fluffy clouds

And then how they darken as they fill to the point

Where they're about to break.

And the rain comes…like tears from a child

Free and unashamed…unabashed…and pure…

Falling down upon everyone. Every living thing

And every dead one as well…

Just falling…washing…cleansing…almost like holiness from heaven

In the way it washes everything.

No matter the creed…or color…or belief…

Or the prejudices they might hold or be built with…

It just falls on everything. Teaching a lesson in the most simple manner

That we have no right to judge anyone.

Oh, yes, we must have laws and some things are just *wrong*

But when it all boils down to it, we can't say that we're any better

Than anyone else

Because you don't know how you would have handled

Their life.

It's so easy watching the rain falling…

It's just in an unjust world.

It makes no divisions…no separations.

It just…falls.

Prei

Mental Stimulation

March 21, 2003

1039

You've never known anyone like me, I'm sure

Don't mean to brag, but sometimes

You have to lay props for yourself

And I'm different…Mister Unusual is a good name to go by

Because my mental capabilities take a different turn

My pleasure is found in the steam building

The teasing and testing

Of the opposite sex.

I can't help but to speak softly and to compliment

On the truths I see

For I don't view flesh, I view souls.

My dark, dark chocolate eyes don't see the skin

But the heart that beats inside those breasts

Rising, falling, full and ripe like fruit for plucking.

Any man can chase a skirt

Nice hips, tights, trim waist and flaunting it all

But few men realize where the real passions found

Where you can find a woman that will scream your name

Not because they're faking and pretending

But because they can feel your soul expand through them.

But I do.

I know, I can, I have, and I will continue to

Explore the landscape called femininity

As I see fit.

Though…I have willingly limited myself…

My wife is the one I relish in now.

The one that quenches my thirst

All others only get teased, toyed with

And passed on.

But ah! My memory is so alive with the pass

The good and the bad

And I remember the abilities that I now use

To overwhelm the love of my entire life…

You should hear the way she screams when we're loving.

How she releases just from looking in my eyes.

How she clings to me so tightly, moving her hips just right

The way she calls for me with her body…telling me it's mine

Without question

Asking me to lay claim to that which will only be her husband's.

Mine.

I'm her's. But mmmm…if you could just look into my eyes a

moment

Stand near, spend time with, and feel me for a second

You'll be jealous of my baby for sure.

Prei

Remembering One's Self

May 15, 2003

0916

I know you don't want to hear it

Pen tips setting fire to old ways and ideas

Step before I decide to

Prei

upon you. My reality is poetry.

It's all I know and all I do

Writing words with more heat than Dragon's Breath

I breathe fire through my fingertips.

I was born to live and not to die

Born to reach past crimson skies

Born to preach and live on love

Born to give it all to the One above.

And I had forgotten about the passion found

When my fingers fly across the keys and touch souls

Words falling from my brain like teardrops of a jilted lover

I'd forgotten the sweet renditions that people sought

The ones that made me worth being sought after

Forgotten about the love of my wife and my friends

And my God

Forgotten because others made decisions

That were good for them and not for me.

But we live our lives for ourselves, again, forgotten

That I have to do what is right for me.

One thing that I should have never forgotten

Is the strength and the power God placed in my poetry.

Praises be due to the One above, because I remember now

And I stand on the throne of Kings and Emperors

I stand above with Phoenix like wings

I stand because I can remember where I came from and how I got

here

And the words that God gave me to bring me thru.

Hail to the King called Christ.

Hail to the One called God.

Hail to the Holy Spirit that edifies.

Hail to them all that made me

God's son.

Prei

What's In A Name?

May 15, 2003

0930

My name is Michael, meaning

"He who is like God."

Yet I am just a man

With frailties and shortcomings.

I make mistakes and I slip in my promises

Sometimes I don't come up to even the standard

I wish to hold myself to, let alone God's.

Yet I have been given a name that tells me

Of potential.

I have been given the name of an Archangel

The very one charged with kicking Lucifer out of heaven.

I have been given the name of a warrior, a fighter

The name of a Lover, a Master

And ultimately a Judge.

I have been given a name that means I must be better

Than even I think I can be.

A name that calls me higher than I ever wished to be.

And though in truth it is just a name

The meaning behind it, the power in the Word itself

Makes it more than that. It makes it a label. A title. A position.

It becomes who I am and who I will be.

It encompasses me, and no matter what I call myself

Be it Prei, Mike, or Micah

Michael…that one word that made me…*me*

Will always be who I am

Lest God should change my name.

Prei

<u>Resurrection</u>

May 18, 2003

0215

Without pain, there is no change.

Without *sacrifice*, there is no growth.

Only through the embracing of death to one thing can we become
another.

Just like a seed, our life begins…

We are born, we breathe, we exist in visible, tangible form.

Our hearts beat, pumping blood

To nourish the electrical impulses of our minds…

Yet we are only beginning.

We are then just seeds, planted in the soil called Life

Nourished by the waters of Experience

Just getting started.

And we grow. We do all those baby things

From not being able to hold our heads up

To holding our heads up high.

From crawling to walking to running

We grow.

And then we die.

We die to our childishness.

We learn that the world is not such a nice place after all
And that boogey men do exist.
There is a monster under the bed
And it's out to pluck us from our soil prematurely…
We come face to face to that thing that kills our innocence
Called Living…

The sadly ignorant among all of us succumb to it
Never realizing that we, like the seed
Transcend Death.

For the seed dies so the plant can come forth.

Childish innocence parishes to allow the man (or woman) to take root
in this world.

Thus, we begin the process of sacrifice
To continue on to the next phase of Life.

Learning we cannot have everything we want.

That not *everyone* will like us.

Sometimes your best friend becomes your worst enemy.

Your first heartbreak.

Your first true love.

Your first kiss, first "touch," first sexual experience…

…All rings on a tree, growing…each a cycle of life then death, then life again…

A continual process that molds us and shapes us into who are *now*.

Not all painful, but all changes
That end one phase of Life to start another.
And only the weak
Or the foolish
Or the lazy
Or the dumb
Get trapped in one phase of existence.

Life without change is a constant Death
And those in that state of existence are an abomination
Called the Undead.

You are what you are and what you were and what you will be

All at the same time.

You are only living and dying to move from one place to the next in

eternity

For we are eternal beings trapped in

Time.

Even Jesus died and rose again before saying

"All power in Heave and Earth is in My hands"

And He never once stopped being

The Son of God.

Prei

Poetic Outlook

<u>Silver and Gold</u>

December 31, 2002

1553

This is about my pistols,

The pens that I use,

To write my verses and my rhymes,

Gold-plated Lyrics,

Silver-plated Verse,

To spread what I'm holding,

Here,

Within me.

Sometimes violently,

Sometimes in melody.

Either way the shots they fire

Are meant to aid.

Sometimes they must harm you,

To do the good they're meant to do,

Most times they just loose you

From the chains that bind,

And twist,

And lock down the heart.

I've been blasting them for years now,

Every chance that I can get,

And one day they'll be my living,

God said…

But whether that's today or tomorrow,

Or years down the road,

I'll keep using my pens,

Emptying the clips to my pistols,

Gold-plated Lyrics,

Silver-plated Verse.

The Rajamalan,

Mj Omega

Just Flowin'

January 7, 2003

1224

I need to just release…

To lay back and to let my mind fall into

An easy-listening environment,

Relaxed and falling in love with the sounds

Of the jazz coming through the speakers.

Just what I need today,

A moment to let go of all my troubles and just slip away

To a Neverland of existence,

A place only found behind the starts

And just left of the moon,

Glowing beside the sun.

Each beat of the drums plays in my head,

Matches to my heartbeat,

Bum-ta-ta-tum…smooth and easy…

And the melodic sounds of the piano and sax

Bind together to make love to my soul…

I'm transported to the smoky club scene,

In a small, quiet, hole in the wall,

Located in the middle of nowhere…

'Cause see, it's out there that the jazz plays most lively…

It makes you bob your head and tap your foot,

Yet somehow it causes you to also…disappear…

Into your own personal world of bliss.

It takes me where I need to be…to a place where my pen

Can hit the paper,

And just…flow…

Till the last drop of ink runs out.

The Rajamalan,

Mj Omega

<u>Observance</u>

January 21, 2003

1634

My world…my life…my sense of being…

Is entirely made up of words.

If I were an artist, then they would be my paint.

I could sculpture a model out of them.

In each breath I take, there is a word found…

In each experience, a phrase…

In each instance, a sentence,

And so on and so forth

As I continue with the paragraphs of an hour,

The essays of AM and PM,

The story of a day,

And the poetry of my existence.

I act…I work…I believe…I do *everything*

To back up and validate my *words*

Because in them is my heart found.

In *them* is the core of my soul,

The very breath of life…

Even God himself *spoke*…to create something as beautiful

As mankind was…

And now I, after so much time…continue weaving the fabric

Of life via the power of my *words*.

Miracles in written form words are,

Because though the paper or papyrus may fade,

Though the symbol may change,

Though the very sound might become something different…

A word remains a word,

And its mark will always somehow be remembered

Even if it's origin is lost.

The Rajamalan,

Mj Omega

Exposed

February 7, 2003

1656

Laid out before me, spread wide, spread open

There are no restrictions to what I see. There is nothing to stop me

From tasting of your being. Sipping your soul.

Poetess! Pour yourself out before me!

Wet the sheets with your words

Soak the atmosphere with the dampness of your scent

Let that flavorful fluid drip upon the pages…

One word, two words, three!

Write for me, poetess! Write me true poetry!

Tear it from your heart and put it before me

Make me look and see the beauty therein!

Capture my attention with lines, lyrics, verse and prose

Make love to the imagination!

Prei

PREI

Visual Stimulation

February 10, 2003

2312

Lines read slowly, bit by bit

While the mind opens like the sun blinking on the horizon

Sparkles of intelligent flood the brainwaves

Synapses snap with the tension

Mental abbreviations rumble through me,

Yet I read. I read each glorious word while my soul reaches out,

Entangling itself with every phrase and prose.

Every moment builds upon itself until finally…

Finally I sit back, exhausted and breathing heavily,

Mentally orgasmic…

Shivering with the aftershocks of poetry.

Prei

PREI

Kiele's Mask

Down With the Kings!

December 24, 2002

1010

I came in, silent,

Like a whisper,

Like darkness creeping through the evening,

With a soft caress and sweet word,

Trying to feel, trying to see,

Trying to seek out some locked up *essence* of,

Myself,

And my world…

Feeling drawn,

Feeling pulled,

Tossed even,

Into this place,

Where Kings and Queens sit upon various thrones,

Their crowns glowing and heads held up high,

For their kingdoms were well fought for,

Established,

By their power with the written word.

Each a force to be reckoned with.

Each an adversary to face.

Each being the best friend you could have,

A sounding board to hear your words,

Your world,

Screamed back at you,

Be it good or bad.

Each being regal, and with head held up high,

Not for false bravado,

But for the swell in their hearts,

And the pride in their souls,

Each saying; "See me! Feel my spirit!

Feel all of me in every verse,

Every prose,

Every poem that you see,

That flowed like blood from my fingertips,

Into the keys or pens of trade.

See me!"

And so I roam this land, taking notice,

Astounded,

And inspired,

To soar like we will when Christ returns,

Mounting up on the wings of eagles…

One day I will sit upon a throne…

One day I will survey my lands and my kingdom,

And I will proudly proclaim in a voice out loud,

For all to hear and reckon with,

And *tremble* beneath the very intensity of it…

That I too am now…

Down

With

The

Kings!

The Rajamalan

aka

Mj Omega

<u>Young Gun or Verbal Blasting</u>

December 24, 2002

1100

I carry twin pistols,

One in each hand,

Verse and Lyrics.

With Verse I put bullets in your brain,

Of prose and poetry,

Enlightenment,

As I ventilate your mind,

And the air blows out old,

And musty ideas,

So that new thinking can flow.

Lyrics riddles your body,

Putting slugs in your chest,

Stopping your heart with the sensual sounds,

And melodies I can produce,

Blam! Catch that,

A double blast from my twin pistols,

Cocked and loaded at all times,

To unleash the torrent of smooth flowing,

To righteously rearrange your psyche,

To mess up your mind,

To open your soul

To the power of my poetry…

Twin pistols cocked and loaded,

Ready to fling hot lead,

Composed of the thoughts and ideas,

And expressions of *my* life,

To open you up to *my* experiences,

To show you how *I* am viewing things.

Verse.

Lyrics.

They sit by my side,

Weapons of my warfare,

This King of prose before you,

This Priest of passion,

I come, both guns blazing,

Ushering in the new era,

Not erasing the old,

But rather building on and with,

Learning from and teaching,

Expanding altogether to overtake the *world*,

Here I come…pistols cocked back and loaded…

A Young Gun.

The Rajamalan,

Mj Omega

<u>Ode to the Young Guns</u>

January 12, 2003

0754

Slip in the clip, pull back the chamber,

One in the hole, now you in danger,

Verbally slaughter, all in sight,

Crush your mind, help you think right.

Man, bringing the pain, with two pistols,

Pens in my hands become instrumentals.

Rearrange your word pattern, become mental,

Crack the stone heart open, it's essential.

Testing my flow? Boy, you trippin',

I'm a poet for sho; put you missin'

The point in my game, ain't about dissin',

But about bringing a change. Stop and listen.

I'm putting on the mask, Kiele's finest,

Fulfill the task, Young Gun righteous,

We can all see, who's the tightest,

A KM'er I be. Now rewind this,

Slip in the clip, pull back the chamber.

Jack you all up, like a coat hanger.

Put a few in your chest, heartbeat wavers,

Now join the rest that sought danger.

I'll tell you one time just who you face.

Try to run on us? You loose the race.

Young Guns the title. We burn just like mace.

In all our recitals, our flowing, we lace.

WE'RE YOUNG GUNS.

The Rajamalan,

Mj Omega

<u>Predatory Instincts</u>

The Lurker

March 20, 2003

0151

There is within me

A shadow.

A creature lurking in the

Depths of my being

Quiet except for its needs

A *hunger* for eroticism.

Such a thing resides in all truly GOOD men

And it is what causes them to engage

In the physical gratification

Of those they open their hearts to.

Those that seem to need it

Want it

Or know no other means of caring

Than with spread legs.

Each engagement in such activity

Causes it to grow stronger

And to hunger more

Until you teach yourself the words

That stick to women's brains

And cause skirts to go missing.

You fool yourself into thinking

You're doing more good than harm

That you're only fulfilling a need

That *this* is what these hurt women want…

They'll even back your story

Desperate not to lose that small…

Little…

Miniscule amount of love

You show them.

I know, because I've been there.

I've walked those paths and roads

Leasing my heart for sexual release

Picking up the sickness of my partners' soul.

I got to the point wherein

Me and my shadow stood as

One.

An accepted part of my existence

Which I effectively named

My Beast.

Not an odd name for such a part of me

Carnivorous in its pursuit of feedings

Selling pieces of my soul for an opportunity

Of gaining nourishment.

It twisted all my good aspects

Tainting them to devious endeavors

While I struggled for some control

Some reclamation of a body going madly out of

Its mind...

Yet, never thought of my faith as an answer

Tried to solve it myself...

I was a Man! I made the rules to my life

Only to much later find out what a boy I was.

I believed the Internet held the key

For there I could let my words become the claws

Of my predatory nature

And who would I be hurting?

No one.

No disease, no children

Isn't cyber-sex great?

Dark times came for a struggling God's child

Got so good at it that I knew my words

My charm

My personality

Would / could gain me access to nearly any panties

I saw fit to have.

But there was a problem…

A small, overlooked detail.

I cared.

I gave a damn about what happened to those I preyed upon

Though I drank from their wells

I tended to their hearts

And bled constantly from my own.

I created a hell based on lust but made its key out of love

Thus trapping myself inside

For one cannot exist with the other.

And I have suffered…God, how I have suffered!

For misuse of this gift I am given

For I find a reason to Love

Everyone

Even if it's only because God said to do so.

I love in spite of…and only recently have I left my self-imprisonment.

I faced my Best, which had grown into a Dragon

Picked up my sword and with the strength

That my *Wife* gave to me

I slayed that fire-breather

Sealing its death with

God's anointing.

But I still feel its memory

Kicking...

Slipping up on me every now and then

Looking to feed to its point of rebirth.

Yet, I resist...for I am

Prei...

I am the predator that knows how the prey feels

Thus has my reasoning has been

Changed.

Prei

Territorial Markings

March 20, 2003

1207

There are lines drawn, invisibly

Marked so that things that are only palpable

To the senses.

Whether it's a dog pissing on a tree

Or a lion's roar

A boundary is set up, territory is set aside.

Doing such a thing makes the one that marks the land

Responsible for its care

Its upkeep

And its well being.

Defense of that land falls under that cloak

So be sure you're able to hold on to

All that you claim as yours

Before making promises.

Each person you let in

To walk the halls of your soul

Leaves footprints.

Dare they touch your heart

A tether is formed

And in some way, at some degree

Depending on the stronger one

Someone becomes part of another's territory.

Warnings go out quickly

"Don't do that or I'll get you"

Protection is handed out

Others wanting your

TERRITORY

Fighting to lay claim to it

Hearts are wounded

Souls ache

You win some, you lose some

But usually you fight just to maintain and

Gradually gain a larger area of ruler ship.

But be sure you can maintain

Before subjection comes about.

You have to know where you stand

As the leader of the pack

Or a follower of the head.

And know that everybody leads someone
And every leader follows somebody else
Though some places you shouldn't lay your marking
Availability can be scented
By the sensitive.

Prei

PREI

<u>My Pride</u>

March 26, 2003

1840

Wife.

She stands beside me through the thick and the thin

The other half to this King that is already whole

That missing link that makes me, ME

The rib in my side restored.

We are founded in love

Live by God's will

And walk the walk of those that dare to be

One.

No one stands before her

Save the Father, Son, and Holy Ghost.

Twin.

Spiritual counterpart

Call her the replica of my soul.

This woman is like a sister unto me

Close as a brother of my bloodline

Makes me feel doubly blessed.

Love is given, but she can't compare

To the Queen of this pride of mine

Though she knows, and stands and walks and does

All that you would expect and far more.

Now she stands on her own two feet.

Exes.

Various and few

They are whose hearts have been touched

And have caused injury.

Yet breaking a whole hurts both halves

And love was there

Thus caring remains.

They stay of their will

Though I will claim them as a part

Of my, part of my pride.

Each is Queen to another Lion

So rights and privileges are limited.

Friends.

They change. Some go and some stay

The true ones stick beside me

The others can fade in the light of truth.

Kiele's

People that I know and soon others will hear about

They are the poets and poetesses that march out of the shadows

And some of them…heaven, some of them hit me so deep

With words and personality that poetic souls

Are only capable of producing.

They are the soul my writing grows in

They must be counted amongst mine

And me amongst theirs.

Prei

Dominance

April 2, 2003

1657

I…can't hold it back any longer

My blood is pumping hard in my ears

Heart beating against the walls of my chest

I NEED this…

I MUST have this…pleasure

This moment of overtaking passion

This…feeding…I

MUST

Calm this crazing in my flesh

And YOU are the key…the meat that will

N o u r i s h ME

Long into the night.

Forgive me because I'm about to get

VICIOUS

Turn up the juice on the lovemaking scale

And just go for *sex*

Everybody needs some serious, straight out, rock the bed

Headboard knocking, screaming at the top of your lungs

till the neighbors call the cops

LOVING

That kind that makes you ill afterward, not just weak

Makes you feel like you've lost your sense of self and just became

One...**solid**...orgasm...

So, I'm sorry for pushing you all up against the wall

Hands pinning your arms back

I don't need you TOUCHING me right now

Feels like I'm going crazy

Struggling but quickly getting out of these clothes

I hope you're ready...hard to maintain any sort of

Decency

Gotta rock you, right NOW.

Keep your legs around my hips when I lift you up

Let the only thing between you and the floor be my

S T I F F N E S S

That's penetrating and pushing into you deeply

Love seeing those breasts bounce from the force, but just wait

Till later

Because I'm just warming up and this King

Call me YOUR MAJESTY

Is just getting started in the consumption of his

QUEEN.

Keep taking every thrust you receive

Keep crying out for more

Keep driving this wildness on

Till we set the place on fire with the

Friction

Of our motions.

Uh, mami; hold tight while I sling you from the wall to the bed

Laying you on your back, but not getting on top of you

Just standing there, feeding your moist, lower lips inch after inch

Of myself

While you feed me your wiliness to my toy

My plaything

While you let yourself fall into a submission that only can be birthed

From a strong lust

And a stronger love.

Keep your legs right up against me, and closed

Love the way that feels, tight, even more than usual

No problem getting in though, I was built to last

And you're built to surpass every other woman

That crosses my path or eyesight.

Can you stand it? Are those tears of pain or pleasure

Or both?

And does it matter?

What more will this man do when the NEED overruns his rationale?

It's going rampant in my head

Yeah; BOTH of them

And I have to let you see, feel, partake and enjoy

Yeah; BOTH of them

Playing games with you when I lay you on your side

And make you pull your knees up

Didn't know I could do like this, darlin'?

Don't worry…keep pushing my limits and you'll see just

WHAT

I'm capable of.

S t r e c h your legs open now so I can climb on top

Your thighs on mine while I keep you spread

Thrusting, thrusting, thrusting

THRUSTING

Till your nails have left lines down my back from the power of it all

Just about ready, but needing something else…

Put your mouth on me; wrap those lips around me

And pull powerfully until you can feel the stream of life

Rush from the tip of my divine staff

The Japanese call this release "the rain and the clouds"

So let me *rain* on you a bit, before your back bends

And your hips rise in the air, soar; used lips extended

And for a second receiving

Of my fullness. God, I love your operatic sounds

If I could have you like this every day, I WOULD

But my mind can't take the stress that FRENZY

Puts me in

Put me IN, lovely woman

Take me IN all the way while your hips are gripped

And smacked

And bounced

And your insides are turned into fire from the HEAT

That's coming off of me.

Just a sec, let me pull out, put that tip to the clit

And hear you scream about how HOT it is

Glad you enjoyed it

Back to the riding.

Flip, switch, don't miss a beat

You on top now, let you have this place for a moment

Mount your throne, Queen

And throw it on me so hard that all I CAN DO

Is give it back to you

THROW IT till you're tired

Till your back hurts from the way your hips have been flung back

THROW IT on me to the point where if someone was video taping

They'd have to say

DAAAAAMMMMM*********

And keep going till you collapse

But don't think I'm letting you free

Because switches have been flipped already and I CAN'T STOP

I've got to make you lie on your back again and take me in

While your breath runs short and you look at me pleading

Begging for me to stop

Crazy expressions are in your eyes

But that's alright, just stay with me till

The second coming.

Prei

Dedications

<u>To Have Been Your Muse</u>

December 23, 2002

1310

(written for Dustee Larson aka Starrlight12)

If I could have been the subject of your prose,

Not because of my verse,

Or my feelings,

Or anything less,

Than the fact that you saw me,

And perhaps a glimpse of my soul…

That is a wonderful gift.

To be basked in the radiance of your words,

To feel the emotion from afar,

Like a cool breeze through the park's trees,

What a great thing!

To be looked upon as a creature to be adored,

To be loved,

To be cherished,

By someone whose soul cries out,

In pain,

In sorrow,

In joy,

In happiness,

In love,

To be a muse for someone like that…

To be that inspiration,

To be that force that moves the hand,

That holds the pen,

Which will write the words that will last a lifetime…

To be *that* is a goal,

Worthy of pursuit.

The Rajamalan

Beautiful Sistas

February 3, 2003

0916

My beautiful, lovely, talented, attractive, sensual, sexy sistas…

Fine like summertime on the beach,

Waves of crystal blue water breaking on the shore,

Sand white as snow, fine and smooth.

My sistas. Intelligent, thoughtful, insightful, wise, sistas…

You remind me of springtime.

Everything new…soft…*gentle* to the touch,

All your senses happily fuzzy with the feeling of life in the air,

All things temperate to the point of rightness…

Perfection.

My sweet, sweet sistas. Loving sistas. Caring sistas. Stick by your side

Sistas.

You're that portion of us that we can't do without,

The proverbial rib that's missing in our bodies.

We are off-balance without your presence, our center shifting to thoughts

Of how to fill the void within us…

That your absence creates.

We rail against you because we know your power…

Because we know what you're *capable* of, given chance and
opportunity.

Sometimes it inspires us that God would create something wondrous

Just for the sake of helping us to meet the goals of life…

For you're our crutch when we feel we can't stand,

Support when we feel we can't make it.

You're there to just be there when we feel all alone in this world…

You're our anchor when things spin out of control.

My Black Sistas.

My White Sistas.

My Hispanic Sistas.

My Cuban Sistas.

My Asian Sistas.

My Sistas of all the creeds, colors, races, and ethnicity,

All over this planet…in every corner of the globe.

This one goes out to those that are…sistas…

May God bless you to be with us, *always.*

The Rajamalan,

Mj Omega

<u>Cross-dressing Woman</u>

February 5, 2003

1308

Venomous chick, spitting poison from between your lips,

Fatal tongue, dropping words like acid on the weary souls,

Who do you think you are? Do you think I don't see you,

Don't feel you trying to bite me?

But your teeth won't sink in, my skins thick like armor.

I'm covered by stronger powers than the vileness in your mouth,

I am resistant. Almost had me there, upset and irritated,

Saying your words as though kind, but laced with deadly substances,

I can sniff the air and breath in the scent of your stench,

Betrayer! Heartbreaker! You who walk with lamb's skin covering your

Hideous exterior. Prior to your belief that all men would fall,

Beneath the spell of your sexiness,

I learned that all girls are NOT created equal; you've got women, and ladies,

Down chicks and then females like you baring a name I won't say,

For fear of losing my Christianity.

Did you think your flat behind and open shirts that bare breast that only look sizable,

Because you're a walking stick figure,

Would truly hypnotize me? Surely you're joking,

I've been jocked by better, resisted *better*,

Been around far better than you.

Beauty running skin deep, your soul is barren though,

Feelings worn on your shoulders, every day raving about another drama,

Shut your mouth! Crossing lines with me that'll have me revved and steamed,

Ready to release my own trigger flung words of despair, unchecked,

Cut you down to size and let you see the realness of who you are,

Which is nothing. Shallow being, caught up in dumb guys talking to you,

Falling for the traps of the wolves that hunt for chicks just like YOU,

Easy chicks, chicks that give it up quick, quick, quick,

Get dissed and dismissed and come back for more of the dick.

You're a foolish one, girl…so foolish.

The boy using you like he would a pool table,

Using his stick to knock his balls in your holes,

And you just keep bending, flexing and extending yourself,

Your wealth gone up in the smoke hell, because that's what you're dealing yourself,

Hell in the form of your life.

You've caused me anger, and I want to retaliate, but now that I look at you,

My heart goes out to you…I feel pained,

Despite the way you behave and the shady deals you make,

Because I know something you don't seem to…

You're lost in a vacant mentality, one that scarcely seems to hold on
to sanity,

All because somewhere along the line, you lost your worth.

Oh, you run your mouth and say you're this and that, but your eyes…

Your eyes just speak of volumes of sadness,

And I feel bad for you for that reason…but you make it hard,

Difficult for me to do so…

Gotta stay in the distance, keep myself in check…gentlemanly words
in the mouth,

Attitude dictating I treat you with respect,

Faith dictating I must love you, despite everything about you…

Praying for God to give me the strength.

The Rajamalan,

Mj Omega

Pimp's Payment

February 7, 2003

1217

What's the matter, pimp? Player?

Looking mighty sick these days

Have your ways

Finally caught up to you?

Six females on a chain you kept,

Rep constantly growing

Got people envying you, trying to be you.

Silliness. You just laughed at them and kept steppin'

Question, though. Did you really think that they were only your

hoes?

Come on; let's be serious…if you're hitting it like that, so easily,

Somebody else is too. You think they're just going to let you hit each

one,

Know about it, and be faithful to you? Ha!

You're not a man…you're just a wolf with a pack of female dogs,

Each one suited for your scoring.

Didn't think they'd bring home the virus though, did you?

Not while you kept cutting raw, sliding into one wet slot after the

other,

Unmindful of the sin you're committing and the punishment for the

crime

Seems death comes swifter for some than others.

Your number's checked.

Do I feel sorry for you? Despite myself, I will admit, yeah…

I really do. I'm hurt to see another man behaving like a boy

Hurt to see the women he's left marked, lengthening the scar across their hearts

I'm hurt to think about how you might have infected after you caught this

Hurt to see ladies behave like whores.

I know how you're feeling, man…I know you're wondering how this happened…

Just having fun, right? I like fun too…my penis doesn't have to be involved though.

Worried about what to do? Well, if I were you I'd make sure things were in order

Especially with your soul. See, God will always forgive those that ask sincerely

But some seeds we sow just have to come up…you may or may not be healed…

Can't tell you, I'm not God.

But I can tell you this…for the things you've planted and the seeds you've sown

Despite how it might hurt to see another suffer…this is the payment you asked for.

Prei

<u>Many Thanks</u>

April 1, 2003

0956

This is a thank you

To all those ladies out there

And to my brothers

That look upon my words as something

Wonderful

Enchanting

Enriching

And worthy

Of reading.

For everyone that looks at the things birthed in me

And finds a value in them that calls their own soul

Into a unity, whether such lines be born of ink and paper

Or fingers and keys

Thank you.

You don't know how much encouragement you lend to me

How you make me feel, how you strengthen my resolve

To keep writing, keep reaching

Keep striving for my dream.

You don't know the influences you have on me

To refine my writing

Change the style up a bit

Re-work the norm into something new…

Different

Uniquely me.

If I could shake the hands and give hugs to my brothers

All of them

I would.

If I could kiss the cheeks and embrace all my ladies

I would.

But I cannot…not now, at least. Maybe one day…

For now, all I can say is Thank You.

From the bottom of my heart and the depths of my being

Thank You.

I've had strange encounters that were glorious in themselves

From those that tell me I'm teaching them

To those that wish to stand beside me just because of my words.

Even that one that always looks at my writing with such intense

interest

That I am wowed by the effect it has…

All of them, and all of you, and all of those I don't even know about

Thank You.

You make a young poet feel like a master of his craft already.

Prei

<u>**Baby**</u>

Loving You

January 22, 2003

1122

Loving you…do be do be do,

It's like a song playing in my head.

It fills me up and fills me out,

For I *expand* with the knowledge of it,

And the feeling.

I spread out like a set of wings on a 747,

Or an eagle,

And I *soar.*

Loving you…wow…it's like…

A totality. See, you begin here,

And I end there,

So that we two become like Alpha and Omega,

Standing in a completion,

Breaking up mathematical equations,

Because with us 1 plus 1 equals

One.

Loving you…blinding side effects,

It turns me upside down and seems to open my heart,

Refusing to take no for an answer as if I would dare say that!

It steps in and beats with each ba-dum of my heart,

Filling my soul like blood fills my body,

And you become a living, breathing, part of my very existence

Because you see, baby,

Loving you…that's like ice cream on a hot day,

Or cool lemonade when you've come out of the sun,

Or just clear, crystal water when you're at the beach,

Wherein you see all the little fishes swimming around in schools of

50,

Moving as if in one *breath,*

Even better than the sunrise over the waters or the trees,

Light hitting everything at once, *suddenly,*

Just like *loving you…* it's all good!

It all makes me feel wonderful!

YOU make me feel WONDERFUL!!

You're like a drug to me, baby,

Because you get me *high.*

Clichéd though that statement is,

The truth rings in it.

I just can't get enough of you,

Totally addicted.

Loving you…loving you is like…

Everything.

Because to me you are

Everything.

And I'm willing to give you

Everything,

To prove I love you more than,

Anything.

Loving you, my babygirl, my woman, my wife,

My lover, my friend, my mother, sister, aunt, cousin,

Loving you makes you become, to me,

Everything that I will ever need…and I cleave to you,

Biblically.

I step away from all I know and I hold fast to *you*

Because loving you…*loving* you…

Is only comparable to

Loving you.

The Rajamalan,

Mj Omega

<u>Touch</u>

February 7, 2003

1107

It's like fire caressing me when you touch me

Burning without breaking the skin…

Simmering my soul, not my flesh

You stir me up inside.

Your fingers are the melting ice cube

That trickles down my back

Down the center

Wet…tingling…a sensation that caused conflictions

Pleasure from the chill.

You are like honey upon my tongue when I kiss you

Rich, thick, sweet…

You pour yourself into me, wholly

Straight from the comb.

You drip…like ice cream does in the sun

Causing sticky fingers and happy smiles

You run like water against the shore

Constantly eroding and refining

Defining in the each return.

You become my sunshine…bright, brilliant, blinding

You are my moonlight…soft, quiet, shining

You are my day and night, my companion

You know me…better than you know even yourself.

You are my touch from heaven…my constant reminder…

Of what love is all about.

Prei

I'm Feeling...

February 12, 2003

1246

Hot. That's what going on with me now.

Sitting in this chair, looking around at so much fineness

So much beauty…bouncing behinds strutting

Breasts bouncing and slits in skirts and dresses…

Sex on the very air.

It made me think of my baby…and of the morning day before

yesterday

When she gave me ample reason to wake up.

Felt someone tugging on me…pulling at my shaft

Gone rigid in my sleep…

Curling up next to me, rubbing against me

Lusciousness of breast, big, soft, and upon me

Thigh on my thigh, chin on my shoulder

She was…cooing for my attention.

The girl makes me feel good!…What, with the way she

Beckons to me with eyes of deep brown chocolate

And whispers things that get my blood to boiling…

Sleep was still in my eyes I remember

Contacts, worn thru the night, were too dried out to see properly

But I could tell what was wanted…felt the desire in her hand

As it moved up and down, coaxing and teasing

Pleasure promised with each fingertip's touch.

She…toyed with me…

She…teased me…

She…tested me, tested to see if I wanted her

Was I committed to having her, body and soul?

Was I going to give her my flesh for her own?

Believed, she did, when finally the tip pierced the folds

Wet, sticky, slick…tight…deep…accommodating for me.

Perfect fit.

The rise-fall motion was perfected in the bed once again.

The stroking of things unearthly.

We beseeched the heavens to watch love unfold.

Passion was born from our *hearts* and not our lust,

For when we're loving we wake the neighbors.

We make the dead sit up and pay attention.

We move mountains of doubt against our making it

Drop the fears that something will tear us apart…

For in each thrust is found the seeds of bonding

And every scream gives birth to an understand

That loving like this…like *this* is not a trivial matter.

When we love like…this…we hear each other's hearts whisper

"I love you" and "I love you, too."

Large nipples became the breakfast

Washed down with the cries of climax

Pulsing inside her, driving her over the limits

Screams heard so loud between 6 and 7 in the morning

For my name stayed on her lips while I stayed

In her arms

Feeling like my heart had split open and all the love I had inside

Was rushing out...

Hand placed over my chest, seal restored

Overwhelmed and caught up in this that only we two share

Denied all others, special gift we give to only one another

Caused my day to run smoothly for two days now...

Women got me thinking about how they try but can't hold a candle

To the light in my baby's eyes for me

Or the light in mine for her...

Revealing clothing sells sex to my mind

As others try to capture our infinite understanding

We will be...*forever*...

And all they are doing is making me think about her

And that morning two days ago.

Prei

For the One I Love

March 11, 2003

1531

Sometimes I wonder if I do enough for you

Whether I show enough love and affection

Whether I give you the friendship you need

And the arms that should hold you when you're hurting

Or just want to cuddle.

I even wonder if my pen drops ink to pages

Or rather if my fingers move the keys along

To produce the flowing rhythms that would tell about you.

Sure I've written words for others

Based on more carnal things and romance of man

But with you it's different…

See, you are my poetry.

You are the source of my words, because you are my heart

And whether I'm writing romance or about pain

I must tap into

My Heart.

Thus, everything written for anyone else is just second-rate material

Because the first place ribbon is pinned on you.

Though sometimes I wonder if I show you that enough…

Whether if I tell you enough that…

I love you.

Prei

This Is For My Baby

March 17, 2003

1409

I get so lonely

Sitting at this desk

Working quietly, minding my own…

I get lonely because I'm not around you.

I don't have you to hold in my arms

Or feel a sweet caress from…

I don't have you close enough to me to kiss

Just for sake of the kiss

Instead, I find I'm just left to ponder and think

About how wonderful it will be

When I never have to leave your side for anything

Except the occasional bathroom break.

Only you know the REAL me…

The changes that others have caused

The person that I am and that I can be

Only you bring the best in me…

Those absolutely shining qualities

That you can see so easily with a glimpse of my eyes

Only you can take away this type of loneliness.

The type that makes me feel like I must occupy myself

Or go crazy thinking about you.

My heart, my soul, my exceptional lover…

My darling, dearest, most beautiful and wonderful everything

I love you.

And I miss you.

I need you.

And I want you.

And I will always be lonely

When I'm not with you.

Prei

We Stand Together

March 19, 2003

0911

Looking up to the sky, time for a testimony

Because God's been blessing me despite my shortcomings

Dropping anointing on me like grease falls from the frying pan

Hot to the touch but capable of making something great

Out of something that's poisonous in its current condition.

I stand up and I look ahead. I see the demons coming

But I've battled these before,

Won some

Lost some

But I'm still here and ready to battle again.

Tried to do it in my own power

Swing of the fist, kicking with my legs

Tried to hold my own, but then saw I was fighting the wrong battle

And looking like Mike Tyson battling Lennox Lewis.

Caught a punch to my soul that made me fall so low

Forgot about God's promises for a moment…felt forsaken

But my eyes have seen the glory of the coming of the Lord

And though these beasts from hell knocked me down

They only knocked me to my knees…where I can reach out…

Where I can cry to the Father as my memories return

And I see His son spread out there on the cross,

Not because He wanted to be

But because He knew it was the only way we could ever

Return to His love.

It was out of love.

I think I feel my help coming on…

Stood up again, power flowing through my veins

And screamed out like Denzel in Training Day

But with a purpose

"King Kong ain't got NOTHING on ME!"

And let free with a burst from the very heart of my being

Of full anointing.

Slayed them bastards…them who are without fathers

Because they have been removed from Glory

Unredeemable are demons, though people still have the chance

To turn around and try a new path, get a new perspective.

The screams of the hell-born were heard by their master

And he sent a thousand more to combat me.

Felt alone, for all I could see was the opposition

Though I yet battled on…yet did I keep fighting, stumbling, but rising

Swinging a spiritual sword well dressed in spiritual armor

How much could I bear?

Looked up and suddenly there another kind of help on the way

Called Wife and she was blessed in the anointing, walking the walk

And talking the talk

Jumped right in the battled, joined hands with me and the two became one

But because of the characteristics we took on

Unique combination of individuals, both whole but still needing one

another

We had a new strategy: for one may chase a thousand

But two WILL put ten thousand to flight

Can't beat God's mathematics

So we stood like Children of Dune, but flowing in God's power

Roaring, "I will not fear. Fear is the mind-killer.

I will face my fear and let it pass through me!"

Made a step and blurred through the hoards before us till we stood

Alone, but with God, blessed though weary from the battles

Looking ahead to the bright new future made

For the husband and wife brought together by holiness.

Prei

About the Author

This young man is a true hidden talent. He has been writing his whole life, finding that he could better express himself through the written word than the spoken. His outlook is much different than most, and it is through poetry that he invites others to walk through his mind. At the age of 23, the pure expression of his work and depth of his words moves the soul.

www.ingramcontent.com/pod-product-compliance
Lightning Source LLC
Chambersburg PA
CBHW020418290526
45785CB00002B/624